About
Newlyn & Mousehole

Michael Sagar-Fenton

Bossiney Books · Launceston

First published 2000 by Bossiney Books
Langore, Launceston, Cornwall PL15 8LD

© 2000 Michael Sagar-Fenton

ISBN 1-899383-31-X

Acknowledgements

We are grateful to the Royal Institution of Cornwall for permission to reproduce
the historic photographs in this book. The modern photographs are by
Paul White except that on page 7 which is by D Jones and is
reproduced by courtesy of the Isles of Scilly Steamship Company.

Printed in Great Britain by R Booth (Troutbeck Press), Mabe, Cornwall

Penzance Promenade, snaking towards Newlyn in the distance

Introduction

History usually flows naturally from geography. If the south coast of West Cornwall drove in a straight rocky line to the final wedge of Land's End, there would be no human settlements of any size to the west of Falmouth. But instead there is a huge bite out of the granite plateau.

If the bite had been just a little deeper, the soft filling between Marazion and Hayle would have been washed away completely, leaving West Penwith as a remote and hazardous island lying off a new 'Land's End'.

But instead the bite made a large bay, most of it sheltered from the eternal Atlantic gales by a one-hundred-metre high granite wall, leaving – as a grace note – just the eye-catching tidal island of St Michael's Mount. And it provided a safe anchorage, sandy beaches to land on, and the possibility of sea-faring communities.

The significance of this is hard to grasp in an era of land transport. Until the railway age, land travel of any kind was always the last resort, and the sea was the international highway for transport, trade or war. No records exist to tell us of the earliest history of seafaring, and it is not until about 30 BC that the first mention of the Land's End peninsula is found, though the description is based on books, now lost, written by earlier travellers. The Greek writer Diodorus describes a tin-producing community 'especially friendly to strangers and, as a result of trading with foreign merchants, civilised in their dealings.'

Tin was the main draw for these early travellers, but the refuge provided by the natural harbour sheltered many others. The confused winds, currents and tides of Land's End were particularly dangerous for sailing boats, and many travellers chose to land in Mount's Bay and cross the short peninsula to Hayle before taking ship again for the west coast of England or Ireland.

Probably the first place in the bay to take advantage of the passing shipping was the Mount itself. Being a tidal island it was easy to land a boat, load it and float it off again without the need for much more than a wooden jetty. However, there were disadvantages. The Mount is in a more exposed part of the bay, and difficult to land on in hard weather, let alone darkness or fog. As time went on, the calmer north-western corner of the bay became a powerful attraction and a number of small communities grew up there, both to take advantage of the lucrative foreign trade and also as local fishing ports.

Mousehole was probably the first, just a rocky cleft – much like present-day Cadgwith on The Lizard – where boats could be drawn up above high water, but with the additional shelter of St Clements Island, the first real haven for any sea traffic from the west. Newlyn, now the grandest fishing port in the bay, and one of the busiest in the country, was harder to enclose and its heyday came later.

The original 'Pen Sans' or Holy Headland is now the site of the swimming pool – which has itself become a valued historical feature

No doubt the stretch of sea still poetically known as 'Gwavas Lake' between the two villages was as popular an anchorage then as now, being traditionally the stillest area of water between Land's End and The Lizard.

A huge spur of granite extends from the northern hills right down into Mount's Bay, where it causes an undersea hazard all the way out to the beacon known as the 'Gear Pole'. This forms a small bay within a bay. Underneath its protection there was deep water for shipping and little exposure to gales. People too found shelter in its shadow. They built the first of a succession of harbours, and put up a place of worship close to the headland where the granite spur dived under the waves – the 'Battery Rocks', now mostly obscured by the open-air swimming pool. They called it the 'Holy Headland' – in Cornish, 'Pen Sans'.

Penzance

The village of Penzance must originally have clung around its most sheltered corner, where the inner harbour and the dry dock now are, and probably extended no further than the bottom of Chapel Street, New Street, Quay Street, and the slipway.

However, the steep, dark and probably unhealthy harbour area in those early days had no suitable open space for a market to serve the peninsula's growing mining population.

The more level ground at the higher end of Chapel Street clearly provided a better location for a market and so, long before records began, what is now clearly seen as the centre of Penzance (the crossroads where Causewayhead and Chapel Street meet the main east-west road) was established as the trading centre of the community.

This inscribed Cornish cross stood in various positions around Penzance's central crossroads for a thousand years, and can be seen today beside the Penlee House Gallery & Museum, which houses a superb collection of local paintings and writings

In Victorian times, on market days, horse buses connected Penzance with all the neighbouring villages and smaller towns

The concept of a market centre – often a 'churchtown' village – separated from its own port is widespread in Cornwall. Sennen and Sennen Cove, Mullion and Mullion Cove, are two other local examples, while Paul and Mousehole have the same relationship in everything but name.

After the Saxon conquest of Cornwall, the Penzance market area became part of a large manor owned by an absent Saxon lord called Alward. Alward's land was taken over by William the Conqueror's half-brother Robert, and much of it fell by diverse means into the Duchy of Cornwall. But his name lives on, as 'Alward-tun' ('Alward's village') changed over the years into 'Alverton'. Although Alward probably never set foot in Penzance, he is associated with a school, a housing estate and a large part of the west of the town.

Penzance, then, became a dual-purpose town practically from the beginning: a port and a market that were too close together to develop into separate communities and too far apart to become completely integrated. Chapel Street, which might have linked them successfully with shops, became a suburb of the port, a collection of fine houses and hotels.

Instead, the shops spread from the market place down the approach road to the east which led towards Marazion, formerly called 'Market Jew'. The port, although lucrative and important, was left to those who had business there and was happily ignored by the rest of the town. 'Penzance', wrote a Victorian traveller, 'turns its back resolutely on the sea... there the price of corn will always be more important than the price of fish.'

This segregation paid dividends in terms of prosperity. Sea ports and fishing villages were not considered charming or attractive, until they were popularised by the influx of artists in the late nineteenth century. On the contrary, they were seen as dirty, smelly and dangerous places, full of drunkards, thieves and worse, and were shunned by both the country people and

The harbour today, with the Scillonian *in port*

the middle classes. So, while Mousehole, Newlyn and St Ives were successful fishing communities, they were never popular with 'Society'. Penzance's star, however, rose and rose, and it was the only town with any social standing to the west of Truro.

Whilst the other towns were rooted firmly in the working classes, Penzance had 'airs', a situation not entirely eradicated by the passage of time.

The port may not have been smart but it grew in significance and added greatly to the wealth of the town which looked down on it. It is hard to conceive just how tiny the seaports were before the Victorian building boom. The port at Penzance consisted of a single stone jetty which extended no further than halfway along the present Lighthouse Pier and was regularly damaged by storms. The weather then was no kinder than now, and the hazards undergone by shipping without enclosed harbours or docks, relying solely on sails, can only be imagined. And in any case, many merchants preferred to risk the soft foreshore by Chyandour rather than to pay harbour dues.

Penzance harbour developed in the mid-nineteenth century as a centre for shipbuilding and repair. The dry dock, finished in 1880, was an important part of this enterprise

Penzance Station in 1870, at a time when there was still mixed broad and narrow gauge track. The continuous rail link to London revolutionised West Cornwall's economy

Mount's Bay lacks the one crucial element required for the development of a major seaport – a substantial river, and so Penzance could never really challenge Falmouth or Plymouth. But it did its best, and in the confidence of the nineteenth century it made a series of massive expansions: the north pier, named after Prince Albert, was completed in 1847; the south pier was extended in 1855 to where the lighthouse now stands; the dry dock was finished by 1880; and the floating dock was completed as late as 1884.

The floating dock had originally been planned for the north end of the harbour, which would have made better commercial sense, because that is where in 1852 Penzance's first railway station was built. The line provided a direct link to London by 1859. As a result, Penzance's seaport blossomed as never before. It became a busy trading port, commercial dock, repair yard and shipbuilders, as well as the ferry port for the Isles of Scilly. Newlyn's fishermen sent their catches by train to London.

It was not until 1968 that the desperate need for a car park became more important than the declining use of the northern part of the harbour, so half the space was filled in for the motor car – the old harbour walls can still be seen around the edge of the car park. Many locals miss emerging from the railway station to the sight of masts and sails just across the road.

Penzance was surrounded by other sizable industrial concerns. Originally these were related only to mining and agriculture, and were restricted by the demands of local landowners and national taxation. Farmers were forbidden to mill their own grain, and were forced to cart it to specified water-mills, making fortunes for the owners. Tin could not simply be sold and shipped abroad, but had to be physically taken to a 'coinage' town to be assayed, taxed and stamped before its sale was permitted.

The privilege of coinage was worth a fortune to a town and was jealously guarded: every ounce of tin extracted from the Penwith peninsula had to be carried on ox-carts all the way to Helston and back. Helston's own small port was continually frustrated by sand and in 1664, in response to repeated petitioning, Penzance was granted coinage town status. This became a third core business to add to the harbour and market.

Local industry grew until, by late Victorian times, Penzance was flourishing in every direction, with huge smelting works, flour mills, warehouses, timber mills, iron foundries, gas works, boat-building, rope-making and other associated concerns. Nurtured by the railway, the market was also at its zenith, able to send fish, fruit, vegetables and, increasingly, spring flowers to Covent Garden within a day of harvesting.

Such success called for appropriately grandiose buildings. The Market House (now Lloyds Bank) was opened on the site of the previous one in 1838, and the 'Public Buildings' (universally known as 'St John's Hall', which is in fact within them) were opened on the western outskirts of the town in 1867.

Numbers 6-7 Chapel Street, much better known as 'the Egyptian House'. This was rebuilt in its present form by a mineralogist called John Lavin in 1835 and reflected the current vogue for antiquities, particularly all things Egyptian. It gradually faded into the background until the 1970s when the Landmark Trust undertook a thorough restoration to its original brilliant colours. Many thousands of people crane their necks from the other side of Chapel Street every year to admire its colour and detail

Earlier detached houses are few and far between in the town. During that period Penzance's fortunes were much inferior to the great mining and industrial towns of Hayle and Camborne, which are now in such a sad state of decline. However there are some elegant terraces to the south and east of Market Jew Street – North and South Parade, Clarence Street and Place, Morrab Terrace and Place, St Mary's Terrace, Regent Terrace and Square, and Chapel Street itself The truly wealthy families, whose fortunes derived from farming, trading, shipping, banking and

Sir Humphry Davy's statue in front of the Market House. He is shown holding the miners' safety lamp for which he is chiefly remembered. Its invention in 1816 allowed a huge increase in the output of the coal mines and helped to fuel the industrial revolution

numerous other enterprises, and whose names appear as a constant strand in the history of the area, shunned Penzance altogether and built their country houses in open parkland ringing the town.

Another famous Penzance name belongs to the man whose figure has been gazing down Market Jew Street towards his home village of Ludgvan since 1872 (often with a disrespectful seagull on his head) – Sir Humphry Davy. He holds in his hand the best remembered symbol of his fame, the miners' safety lamp. This was a simple device which allowed a naked flame to be carried in coal mines without the risk of a methane gas explosion. Davy undertook to solve the problem as a favour, spent only a few weeks working on it, and declined even to take out a patent on the lamp. But it saved unknown numbers of lives and continued in use until the age of electricity.

Davy's main passion was for chemistry, and he was a crucial figure in bringing forward the discipline from its mystical past in alchemy into the precise science it has been ever since. He was the first to isolate the common elements sodium and potassium, he discovered early anaesthetics, and with his assistant Faraday did much of the groundwork towards the use of electricity.

When not involved in researching and demonstrating his work all over Europe, Davy was President of the Royal Society and even found the time to write a book on angling.

As the industrial boom slackened and the collapse of mining led to a mass exodus from Cornwall, tourism began to assume a more important place in the local economy. The railway line ran both ways, and a little genteel tourism became popular with those seeking a healthier climate away from the cities. At first it was only a trickle of the very rich or curious, but Penzance was not slow to take advantage. The Promenade was built in 1844 for visitors to walk along and in 1861 the grand Queen's Hotel was built for them to stay in (thereby blighting the view from much of southern Penzance). It also became fashionable to winter in the West Country.

As tourism gently developed, it brought opportunities for new forms of enterprise. Holiday makers needed to have somewhere to stay, somewhere to eat, servants, transport to local beauty-spots, trips round the bay, entertainment and so on, and all these provided new openings for local labour. The work may have been menial, but in comparison with the other dangerous and laborious alternatives, it was easy.

All that stopped with the First World War, and had recovered relatively little by the outbreak of World War II. Then suddenly the social changes 'up country' created an affluent and increasingly mobile working class. They came west in hundreds of thousands, first by train and then more and more by car. The large Edwardian terraces which had been built to house Penzance's merchant classes with their families and servants immediately turned over to the bonanza of bed and breakfast, run almost entirely by women. Their golden era only lasted through the 1950s and 60s, before tourists demanded higher standards, more space, fewer house rules, and somewhere to park their cars. Tourism became once more a professional career rather than a useful boost to the average family income.

Penzance today is subject to the crisis affecting all of Cornwall. The ancient occupations of mining, fishing and farming are in decline. The only sources of income are tourism and other service industries.

It is in many ways a doleful exercise to compare the bustling prosperous town which entered the twentieth century with the current model. However, although the Victorians were astute at creating wealth, it remained in very few pockets, and the standard of living of the average Penzance resident of 1900 cannot compare with today's.

All Cornish people have learned to be adaptable and resourceful, and Penzance is no exception. The revival in 1990 of the Golowan Festival at midsummer helped create a new sense of civic pride, and Penzance is also provided with a small theatre in a converted chapel, the oldest continuously running cinema in the country (the Savoy – sole survivor of three original cinemas) and a fine tradition of cultural societies. Although it lacks the visual appeal of other Cornish seaports, it has a certain faded Edwardian grandeur, especially when seen from the sea, and it continues to charm visitors and settlers, as it has done since prehistory.

Two faces of modern Penzance: the Barbican area by the harbour (above) and a delightful early Victorian terrace (below)

The harbour and part of the village of Newlyn

Newlyn

Travellers to Newlyn now pass through a continuous run of suburban housing and are hardly aware that they are going from one community to another. But it has not always been like that, for Newlyn was once a collection of smaller villages: the Tolcarne area centred on the old water-mill, Street an Nowan on the lower ground, and Newlyn Town on the cliff around the old harbour. And until the 1930s there were still open fields on the Lidden. Penzance and Newlyn were not only separate but often engaged in open hostilities. A line was sometimes drawn on the centre of old Newlyn Bridge, and woe betide those who dared cross it in either direction.

As a port, Newlyn suffered the penalty of its sheltered position. A steady accumulation of fine mud made for a soft landing place but prevented easy transport of fish or goods (nothing changes – as I write a dredger is hard at work within the harbour). Penzance and Mousehole had deeper, cleaner water and for centuries kept Newlyn in the shade. In 1337, for example, the Duchy of Cornwall's levies showed ten fishing boats in Mousehole for every one in Newlyn.

However, from the fifteenth century onwards Newlyn had a small quay, and gradually its fortunes rose. Mousehole was limited by its capacity and exposure, and Penzance was principally concerned with trade and commerce. Newlyn was a safe haven in almost every weather, and so – pushed along by the huge demand for pilchards – its room for expansion was slowly exploited, despite strenuous opposition from Penzance, including a petition to Parliament. Eventually the vast forty-acre harbour was planned and finally enclosed by the North and South piers at the end of the nineteenth century, thereby unifying the village as we now know it. Even this was eventually to provide insufficient scope for the fishing fleet, and a central pier – the Mary Williams Pier – was erected as late as 1980.

While other Cornish harbours have declined or taken to the softer life of holiday resorts, Newlyn has retained its identity as a working port and is one of the largest fishing ports in the country. This gives the village its own character, a place where the necessities of industry outweigh the demands of the visitor – and where visitors are indeed welcome only as long as they keep in their place. Fishing is a hard and dangerous profession, and Newlyn has an edge, a sense of purpose and an unashamed working-class atmosphere now almost unique in Cornwall. It is a tidal village, never sleeping, but constantly moving to the rhythm of the rise and fall of the water within its harbour walls.

The resolve of Newlyn fishermen was put to the test in 1890 when the long-simmering tension between the locals and the

The Old Quay, with the 'gaps' between North and South Piers behind. The South Pier provides a home for the Tidal Observatory for the whole of the British Isles, where Mean Sea Level is still calculated daily

east-coast fishermen burst into violent conflict over the issue of Sunday fishing. The Newlyn men were mostly convinced chapel-goers, but they had to endure the frustration of watching their 'Godless' rivals returning to port on Monday mornings, loaded down with fish and flooding the market. The fight – in which Penzance sided shamefully with the outsiders – was eventually quelled only by the presence of three gunboats and three hundred of the Royal Berkshire redcoats.

Those who appreciate its real virtues and the incidental picturesqueness of its trade have always treasured Newlyn above more obviously appealing Cornish ports. This led to an unlikely marriage between the fishing community and an artists' colony which 'discovered' Newlyn in the 1880s.

Eminent painters such as Walter Langley, Thomas Gotch, Frank Bramley and, above all, Stanhope Forbes were a group of artists who became known collectively as 'the Newlyn school' and who found their inspiration in the busy life of the port and in the traditional lives and homes of its inhabitants. They recorded the fishermen faithfully. What the fishermen and their families made of the artists is not as well-known, but they tolerated them with curiosity and humour, and were undoubtedly delighted – in such a hard-working environment – when offered money for doing nothing but 'sitting'. In 1899 Stanhope Forbes, with his wife Elizabeth, set up an art school, The Newlyn School of Artists.

The Newlyn Society of Arts still has its headquarters in the Newlyn Art Gallery (formerly known as the Passmore Edwards Art Gallery), although ironically the nearest collection of Newlyn School paintings is in Penlee House in Penzance.

Higher Faugan, the home of Stanhope Forbes (1857-1948), a leading member of the 'Newlyn school' of painters

The old road bridge, closest to the sea

The fishing and art communities have co-existed happily ever since. The artists contributed towards the local economy by establishing the craft of copper-beating, which led to some exquisite artefacts with a still-growing reputation. The Crysede Silk Works were also begun in Newlyn in 1919, before moving to St Ives, and their ground-breaking combinations of abstract art and silk printing are still a landmark of design.

As well as the harbour, Newlyn is blessed with a lively stream, and worshippers at St Peter's approach the church over it via an attractive bridge. Nearby the 'Meadery' was for many years the Gaiety cinema, where several generations of Newlyn inhabitants met their dates on another bridge. A third bridge serves the revived pilchard factory, while nearer the sea there is an old road bridge, an even older footbridge, and the bridge which carries the main road traffic, including the enormous pantechnicons which take the processed fish to the continent, a weight unimaginable to the original bridge-builders.

Mousehole

Mousehole has a combination of size, scale and setting which makes it one of the loveliest harbours in Cornwall, if not the British Isles. Its granite walls, showing clearly their many separate ages of construction, enclose an almost hemispherical harbour around which the village enfolds itself.

It owes its existence to the small stream which cuts a substantial valley at the join between two varieties of rock, and created a space long ago where boats could be hauled up above the high-water mark. On the harsh coast this was enough to form the focus of a community. The fishermen also had the ancient advantage that whenever a shoal of fish strayed into the bay their boats were the nearest and thus the first to profit from it. In the prevailing south-westerlies, they could be at work long before boats from other harbours could beat out of the bay against the wind. Along with St Michael's Mount, Mousehole became the first settlement and harbour of note while Penzance and Newlyn were still insignificant.

Its fishing life stretched from prehistory to the age of steam, when its situation no longer offered an advantage. Even into the twentieth century it was astonishingly successful, its harbour filled from side to side with fishing boats, nets hung from poles leant against the harbour walls and from every other possible eminence. Virtually every house was involved in the processing and packaging of fish. Pilchards were the main trade from late summer to Christmas. They were caught by the millions, pressed, salted and arranged in specific patterns before being squeezed into barrels. The whole village was fully occupied in the work – men, women and children – and the air was thick with the reek of fish-oil and tar.

Mackerel, hake and shellfish from hand-made crab-pots were also staples. It is only within living memory that the bustling prosperous port gradually emptied of fishing boats in favour of Newlyn, and Mousehole accustomed itself to a new life as a tourist destination. Not surprisingly, it still retains a strong sense of community and a hard core fishing population, even if the fishermen now sail from their former rival port two miles along the cliff road.

Christmas celebrations are prolonged in Mousehole by the addition of Tom Bawcock's Eve, the night before Christmas Eve. This celebrates the feat of Master Bawcock who is said to have set sail in a stormy period in late December when all others feared to go to sea and the village was starving. On the twenty-third, having been given up for dead, he returned in triumph with 'seven different sorts of fish' sufficient for all.

These were at once baked into a 'starry gazy' pie (a fish pie decorated by fish-heads sticking up through the pastry, staring at the stars).

Tom Bawcock's noble feat is remembered in 'The Ship Inn' on the anniversary, where Tom is impersonated, starry gazy pie is

The old wharf and steps

distributed, and a good deal is drunk. A song was composed to mark the occasion, and the date is now observed not only in Mousehole but throughout West Cornwall.

'A merrier place you may believe
Was Mousehole on Tom Bawcock's Eve...'

Except in 1981, when Mousehole became the saddest place in Britain. The Penlee lifeboat, manned by eight Mousehole men, put to sea in a dreadful storm on 19 December to go to the assistance of the coaster *Union Star*, which was adrift a few miles to the west. They found the coaster and its complement of eight in a desperate situation, caught in a rocky cove, swept by waves fifteen metres high and unable to be helped by the attending helicopter.

Undaunted, they made run after run beside the coaster, though no one emerged to be rescued. At one point they were picked up by a wave and dumped onto the hatches of the coaster, but they slid back into the water and continued their efforts.

The lifeboat station at Penlee, between Mousehole and Newlyn

The Keigwin Arms, now a private house, was the only building in Mousehole to survive the Spanish raid of 1595

Finally, with the *Union Star* almost on the rocks, her crew at last came out and the coxswain, Trevelyan Richards, of the lifeboat *Solomon Browne*, radioed in to say he had four survivors on board. Shortly after that communications ceased.

The wreckage was soon discovered, and Mousehole then had to come to terms with the terrible loss of its lifeboat and eight of its favourite sons. They are still remembered by an annual memorial service and the dimming of the famous Christmas lights for an hour on every anniversary of the tragedy.

It was not Mousehole's first brush with disaster. On the morning of 23 July 1595 the rising sun revealed four Spanish galleys – a raiding party from Brittany, which was under Spanish control. Over two hundred well-trained and heavily armoured soldiers landed close to Mousehole and proceeded to lay waste to the village, killing one inhabitant and putting the rest to flight. They swiftly set fire to the houses, whose roofs consisted mostly of thatch covered with tarry nets, and soon most of the place was in smoking ruins. They followed the fleeing populace to Paul where they were sheltering in the church, drove them out and fired the church and village also.

The Spanish then took ship again and sailed along to Newlyn, where they landed and imposed the same bitter medicine. Some resistance was offered on Newlyn Green, but the defenders were raked with fire from the ships and the raiding party marched almost without opposition into Penzance, which was also mostly destroyed. The galleys terrorised the bay for three days before skipping out to safety on a friendly wind while Drake was attempting to pass The Lizard.

Only Marazion and St Michael's Mount remained intact from the last recorded invasion of the English mainland. In Mousehole Keigwin House – a substantial stone building with a granite porch – was the only building to survive unscathed.

In all, just three people were killed, but it was a terrible blow to the confidence and security of all. Mousehole never really recovered from the Spanish raid, and began from then on to be eclipsed by the rise of Penzance.

It did, however, become expert in the burgeoning art of smuggling, and its many alleyways, courtyards, cellars and other hiding-places made it an impossible place for outsiders to search.

Side by side with the 'free trade' went a paradoxically fierce religious fervour There had been a small chapel of ease in the village – then known as 'Porth Enys' – since at least 1383. (Porth Enys means simply 'Island Port', and St Clements Island once bore a small chapel of its own, probably a monk's cell. No trace remains and the island is occupied only by thousands of seagulls who roost there every night.)

The mother church has always been up the hill at Paul, but other impressive places of worship were built in the village after the rise of Methodism. John Wesley visited Mousehole several

Exotic and tropical plants are common in Mousehole, where
even figs, peaches and apricots can be found growing outdoors

times. The Mousehole faithful walked up the hill to church, crossing Paul folk walking down to chapel. Did they speak to each other, I wonder?

There is another particularly valuable resource in the village: the unique bird hospital started in 1928 by sisters Dorothy and Phyllis Yglesias in their house on Love Lane. It grew to be such a large concern that it was handed over to the RSPCA, but they gave it up after a few years and it is kept alive today by public contribution.

In 1967 the hospital became the centre of world attention when the oil tanker *Torrey Canyon* was wrecked near Land's End, spilling thousands of tons of oil into the sea where it had a disastrous effect on the seabirds. Sad blackened creatures – mostly Auks like Guillemots and Razorbills – were taken in their hundreds to the centre for treatment, though precious few survived despite heroic efforts from the exhausted staff.

Paul

The fine church of Paul, whose tower for centuries has been a well-known fishing-mark, is dedicated not to St Paul of Tarsus, but to the far more obscure figure of St Pol de Léon, or Paul Aurelian. He came to Cornwall from Wales in the sixth century AD and stayed only a few years before travelling on to Brittany, where he founded the cathedral and town which bear his name.

The village of Paul has such a close relationship with Mousehole that they are virtually two parts of the same community. The 'churchtown' never grew into anything more ambitious than it is now: a perfect example of a small village with a church, a pub, a shop and a sports field. Inside the church the scars of the traumatic Spanish raid can still be seen in the form of two fire-blackened pillars.

A short distance from the village towards Newlyn is a large and clearly artificial hill. This was a spoil tip from the huge stone quarry at Penlee, where over the years half a hillside was dynamited and ground up to form durable gravel and road-stone. A small railway used to run directly to Newlyn's South Pier which was used almost exclusively in its service. The quarry was worked until the 1980s. Since then it has filled up with water to form a spectacular inland lake, in places up to twenty-five metres deep.

In the wall of Paul churchyard is an odd memorial placed there by Prince Louis Lucien Bonaparte in honour of a certain Dolly Pentreath of Mousehole, reputedly the last native speaker of Cornish. Certainly the language lingered last in the far west, but whether fishwife Dolly was a true speaker or whether she exploited her celebrity by breaking into a Cornish of her own devising will never be known.

Another Mousehole resident, William Bodener, who was able to speak and write in Cornish, outlived her by twelve years, but it is Dolly's fame which persists

Lamorna

On the mild Penwith peninsula, any valley the wind cannot reach is always lush with growth, both because of the micro-climate and also because of the amount of topsoil blown into the valley over the years. Lamorna is a striking example. It is a very deep-cut valley with a rushing stream fed by a number of sources rising on the nearby moors.

Lamorna has a small harbour which has been established for centuries, but the cove is really too narrow for it ever to have grown into a port like Mousehole. The sheer cliffs funnel the waves up to a dangerous height in winter storms, and the pier has often been washed away.

Today the harbour greets an occasional fishing boat, and it has also found a new use as a centre for underwater diving; fast inflatable boats swarm around it every summer. Its main purpose before that was to serve the two large granite quarries that are cut into the east side of the valley, in land belonging to Lord St Levan of St Michael's Mount.

The Merry Maidens, a stone circle around 4000 years old, lies within walking distance to the west of Lamorna

The rejected stones were pushed out to roll down the slope below, and the resulting spoil tips remain ungentled by the passing of time. A more typical product of the quarry stands by the side of the coast path, a fine dressed block of granite 1.5 metres high, which somehow failed to make the last boat out.

The quarries famously provided the stone for London's Embankment and, more locally, for Mousehole pier, the Wolf Rock lighthouse, the base of the Humphry Davy statue, and the steps of St John's Hall, of which the top step – a six-metre length of dressed stone – is reputed to be the longest unbroken piece of granite in any construction in the world.

The local pub, away from the cove, is called the 'Lamorna Inn' but is known universally as 'The Wink' – a name originally applied to any small pub in a smuggling area, where just by winking your eye you could order your small ale with a stiffener of French brandy.

To visit Lamorna in the winter is like paying a visit to spring, with its early flowers, butterflies and songbirds, in great contrast to the bare windswept hillsides a few metres above.

Places to visit

Here are just a few of the many worthwhile places to visit in the Penzance area. Opening times are subject to variation.

Cornwall Geological Museum, West Wing of St John's Hall, Penzance (open 10–4, Tuesday–Saturday, April to October). A fascinating geological journey through 5 billion years on earth.

The National Lighthouse Museum, Trinity House, Wharf Road, Penzance (open 10.30–4.30, daily, Easter to October). Sited in the heart of a working dock, the museum houses one of the largest collections of lighthouse equipment in the world.

Newlyn Art Gallery, Newlyn (open 10–5, Monday–Saturday and bank holidays). Dating from 1894, the gallery is a leading venue for contemporary art. Its façade has four *art nouveau* copper relief panels, fine examples of the distinctive Arts and Craft copperwork produced in Newlyn from 1890 to the 1950s.

Penlee House Gallery & Museum, Morrab Road, Penzance (open Monday–Saturday, 10–5, May–September; 10.30–4.30, October–April; last admissions half an hour before closing). Permanent displays feature the social history and archaeology of the area, while a lively programme of exhibitions spotlights various aspects of Penwith's artistic heritage, particularly the Newlyn school of artists.

The Pilchard Works Museum and Factory, Newlyn (open 10–6, Monday–Friday, April to October). An award-winning working museum – Britain's last working salt pilchard factory where you can watch the processes and taste the products.

Trengwainton Garden (National Trust), near Penzance (open Sunday–Thursday, 10–5.30, April–September; 10–5, March and October). Closely linked to the stream running through its valley, the garden (favoured for its cultivation of exotic trees and shrubs) leads up to a terrace with splendid views of Mount's Bay and The Lizard.